ON THE HUNT

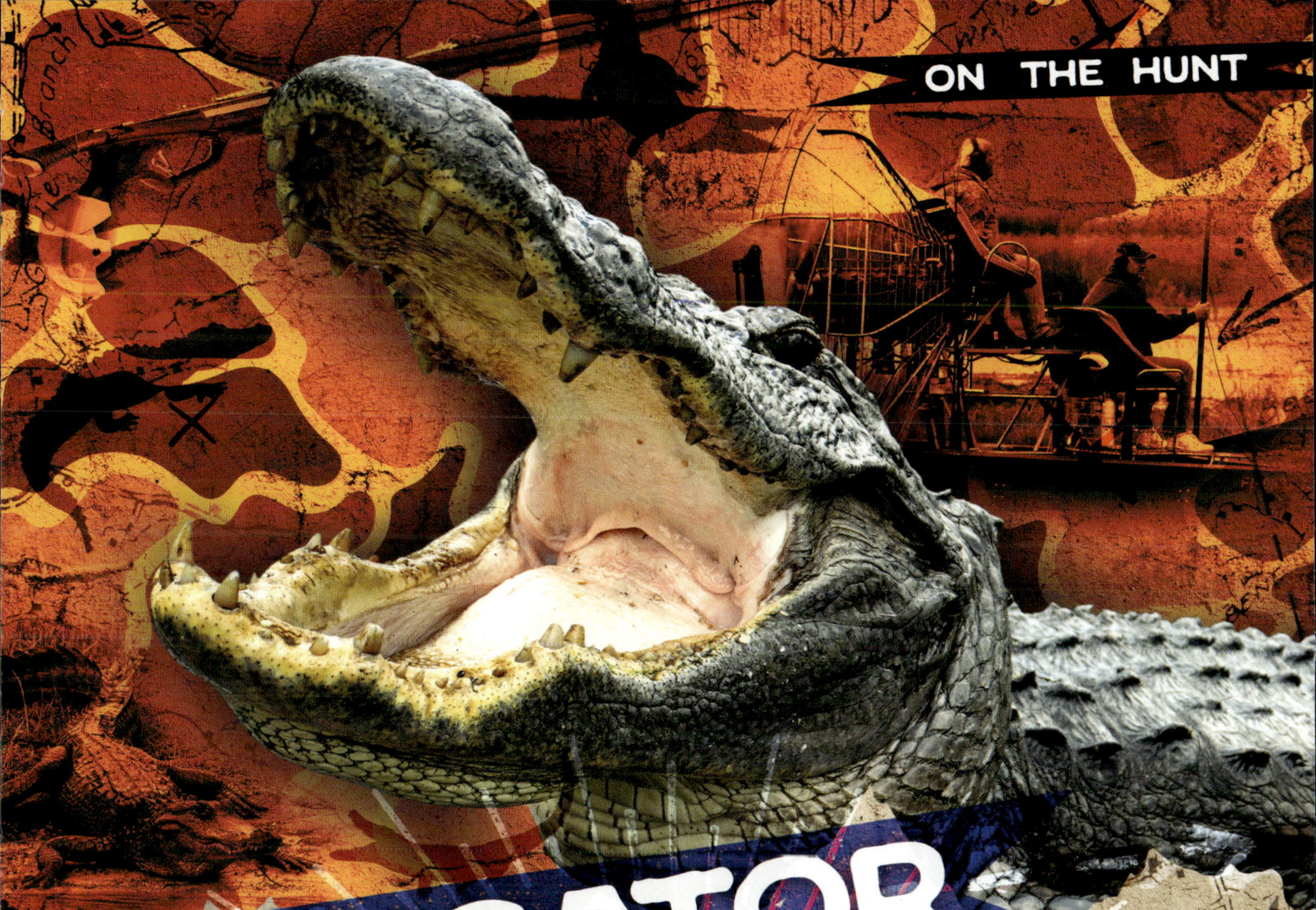

# ALLIGATOR HUNTING

BY ROXANNE TROUP

EPIC

EPIC, AN IMPRINT OF BELLWETHER MEDIA BY FLUTTERBEE

**EPIC**

**EPIC BOOKS** are no ordinary books. They burst with intense action, high-speed heroics, and shadows of the unknown. Are you ready for an Epic adventure?

This edition first published in 2027 by Bellwether Media, Inc.



Library of Congress Cataloging-in-Publication Data

Names: Troup, Roxanne author
Title: Alligator hunting / by Roxanne Troup.
Description: Minneapolis, Minnesota : Bellwether Media, Inc, 2027. | Series: On the hunt | Includes bibliographical references and index. | Audience: Ages 8-12 | Audience: Grades 4-6 |
Summary: "Engaging images accompany information about alligator hunting. The combination of high-interest subject matter and light text is intended for students in grades 2 through 7"-- Provided by publisher.
Identifiers: LCCN 2026001582 (print) | LCCN 2026001583 (ebook) | ISBN 9798898800918 (library binding) | ISBN 9798898802158 (ebook)
Subjects: LCSH: Alligator hunting--Juvenile literature | Hunting--Juvenile literature
Classification: LCC SK305.A44 T76 2027 (print) | LCC SK305.A44 (ebook)
LC record available at https://lccn.loc.gov/2026001582
LC ebook record available at https://lccn.loc.gov/2026001583

Editor: Ashley Kuehl Designer: Jennifer Bowyer

Printed in the United States of America, North Mankato, MN.

# TABLE OF CONTENTS

# MONSTER OR FISH?

People load a boat for fishing. One person carries poles with giant hooks.

Another person brings hunks of meat. They carry two metal spikes. They are fishing for alligators!

# UNDERWATER TARGET

Alligators live in the southeastern United States. Their range covers the Gulf coast, Atlantic coast, and shallow waters **inland**.

# AMERICAN ALLIGATOR RANGE

In most states, people hunt alligators in late summer or early fall.

Hunters use a hook and line to catch gators. It looks like a fishing pole. But **snagging** hooks are large. The line is thick, like rope.

**SAFE**

Alligators were once at risk of dying out. Now more than five million live in the U.S.!

Some states allow hunters to use **bait** while snagging. Others do not.

People hunt alligators for their meat. They make boots and purses from the skins.

Hunters enjoy exploring **wetlands**. They love the action of the catch.

## FAVORITE HUNTING SPOT

### LAKE OKEECHOBEE, FLORIDA

- Home to more than 33,000 alligators
- Huge freshwater lake that covers about **730** square miles (1,891 square kilometers)

fried alligator meat
alligator skin
wetlands

# SPECIAL GEAR

Alligators are strong swimmers. They can hide underwater for a long time. Hunters need a boat to catch them.

A hunter snags an alligator and pulls it closer. A helper uses a **harpoon** or a **snare** to hold the gator.

# HUNTING GEAR

Then the hunter shoots the alligator with a **bang stick**. The hunters wrap the gator's mouth with tape. They pull the gator into the boat and **tag** it.

bang
stick

People often hire guides to hunt alligators. Guides know where to find gators. They know the hunting rules for their area. Many can hunt on **private** land.

# ALLIGATOR TOOTH FAIRY?

Alligators grow and lose teeth all the time. One alligator can grow 3,000 teeth during its life!

# SAFETY FIRST

People must have a **license** to hunt. This limits the number of alligators **harvested** each season.

## GOOD MAMAS

Alligators are in the same animal group as lizards and snakes. Most of these animals do not care for their young. But alligators do. Baby alligators stay with their mothers for about two years.

Some states allow night hunting. Bright lights help hunters find gators. The lights also tell other people where the hunters are.

Hunters should never hunt alone. Alligators are too strong. They twist and fight to escape. They may try to bite. A friend can hold the gator while the hunter makes a clean shot.

# GLOSSARY

**bait**—food used to draw prey to one spot for hunting

**bang stick**—a type of close-range firearm used underwater for hunting alligators and sharks; a bang stick holds only one shot.

**harpoon**—a spear-like weapon with an attached rope that can be thrown or fired from a gun; people use harpoons to hunt large water animals.

**harvested**—collected

**inland**—away from the coast

**license**—a document that gives hunters legal permission to harvest a certain type of animal

**private**—not public

**snagging**—catching underwater animals with a large hook and heavy line

**snare**—a wire loop that tightens around an animal's leg or neck to control its movement

**tag**—to put a paper on the alligator that shows the hunter is allowed to harvest it; a hunter can get tags for a limited number of alligators each season.

**wetlands**—areas of land that are covered with low levels of water for most of the year

# TO LEARN MORE

## AT THE LIBRARY

Mattern, Joanne. *Reptiles: Back from the Brink.* Mankato, Minn.: Black Rabbit Books, 2026.

Somaweera, Ruchira. *The Ultimate Book of Reptiles.* Washington, D.C.: National Geographic Kids, 2023.

Troup, Roxanne. *Python Hunting.* Minneapolis, Minn.: Bellwether Media, 2027.

## ON THE WEB

**FACTSURFER**

Factsurfer.com gives you a safe, fun way to find more information.

1. Go to www.factsurfer.com.
2. Enter "alligator hunting" into the search box and click 🔍.
3. Select your book cover to see a list of related content.

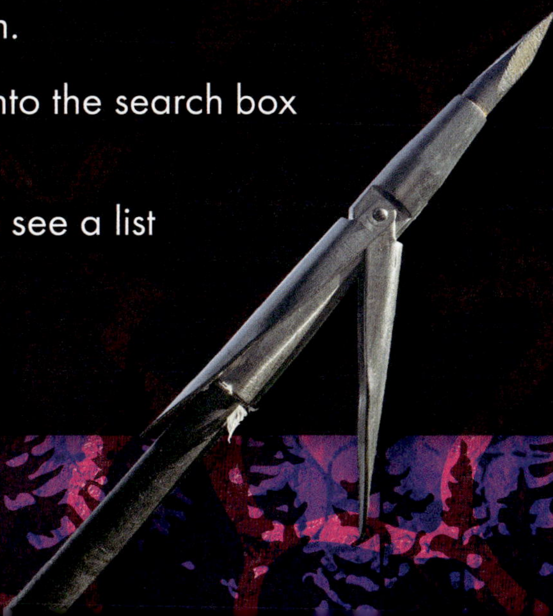

# INDEX



The images in this book are reproduced through the courtesy of: Manuel J. Sachse, front cover, p. 1; ZUMA Press Inc/ Alamy Stock Photo, front cover, p. 1; Jim Schwabel, front cover, p. 1; elenovsky, front cover, pp. 1, 13 (harpoon); reptiles4all, p. 3; Delpixel, p. 4; Stacy Funderburke, p. 5; fotoguy22, p. 6; NNehring, p. 7 (profile); Stephen Molick, p. 7; imageBROKER.com GmbH & Co. KG/ Alamy Stock Photo, p. 8; TrongNguyen, p. 8 (hook); Kristin Elisa, p. 9; Mikhail Anikaev, p. 11; Rakeem Williams, p. 11 (fried gator); herstockart, p. 11 (purse); William and Sons Photo, p. 11 (boots); Delpixart, p. 12; Wirestock Creators, p. 12 (inset); ZUMA Press, Inc./ Alamy Stock Photo, pp. 13, 14 (tag); imageBROKER.com/ Alamy Stock Photo, p. 13 (snagging hook); Kung37, p. 13 (tape); Ron Buskirk/ Alamy Stock Photo, p. 13 (snare); Aleksey Demin, p. 13 (bait); Medard L Lefevre, p. 14; Miami Herald/ Getty Images, pp. 15 (bang stick), 21; Skyfi Media, p. 16; Tosh Brown/ Alamy Stock Photo, p. 16 (guide); Lisa Crawford, p. 17; Richard Ellis/ Alamy Stock Photo, p. 18; Marc Pletcher, p. 19; mark higgins, p. 20; Paulik_by, p. 23.